DAILY LIFE

Stewart Ross

PETER BEDRICK BOOKS
INCORPORATED

ANCIENT GREECE
Daily Life
Gods and Goddesses
Greek Theatre
The Original Olympics

Published in the United States in 1999 by
Peter Bedrick Books
A division of NTC/Contemporary Publishing Group, Inc.
4255 West Touhy Avenue,
Lincolnwood (Chicago), Illinois 60646-1975 U.S.A.

Photographic acknowldgements
The publishers wish to thank the following sources for providing photographs:
AKG London 7, 11, 19, 23, 25, 26, 32, 35, 37, 39, 40;**Ancient Art and Architecture Collection** 17, 22, 28, 41; **C. M. Dixon** 4, 14, 15, 20, 25, 30, 31, 34, 43, 44; **e t archive** 33, 45; **Bridgeman / Ashmolean Museum** 18; **Robert Harding** 44; **Michael Holford** (cover), 8, 21, 24, 29, 36; **Tony Stone** 38-39; **Wayland Picture Library** 5, 45; /**British Museum** 7 (bottom), 12-13, 14, 32 / **Ashmolean Museum** 9.
Illustration: John Yates **Map designs:** Hardlines

Ross, Stewart.

Daily Life / Stewart Ross.

p.   cm. --   (Ancient Greece)

Includes index.

Summary: Examines the history, people, city-states, government, social structure, home and school life, clothing, meals, sports and games, religion, and daily activities of Ancient Greece
ISBN 0-87226-599-4

1. Greece-- Social life and customs Juvenile literature.

2. Greece--Civilisation--To 146 B.C. Juvenile literature.

[1. Greece--Civilisation--To 146 B.C.]   I. Title   II. Series

Ancient Greece (Peter Bedrick Books

DF78.R69   1999

938--dc21   99-18376
                                                                      CIP

Printed and bound by Eurografica, Italy
International Standard Book Number: 0-87226-599-4.

99 00 01 02 03 15 14 13 12 11 10 9 8 7 6 5 4 3 2 1

CONTENTS

1 Into the Agora

Hegeso lies in bed listening to the noises of the dawn. Her mother is still asleep beside her, breathing quietly. From the room next door comes the sound of her father's snores. A goat bleats in the yard outside. Up on the farmhouse roof, a thrush sings its welcome to the rising sun.

Suddenly, Hegeso remembers!

She jumps up and runs wildly around the house, waking everyone with her cries. It's the day she has been looking forward to for ages. For the first time ever, her father is taking Hegeso and her brother Dexileos into Athens with him.

Off to market, about 380 BC. The farmer is using his cheeses as a saddle for his mule.

On the road

Hegeso's father is a farmer. With the help of three slaves, he runs a small farm at the foot of Mount Agaleos, some 10 miles northwest of the city. About once a month, he loads up their mule with goat cheese and takes it into Athens to sell. Normally, he is accompanied only by the slave, Manes. But today he has agreed that once – just once – Hegeso and Dexileos can come, too.

An hour after sunrise, they are on their way. They soon leave the farm track and join the Sacred Way, the main road between their home in the mountains and Athens.

Into the city

They cross a large river, and Hegeso's father points out the *Acropolis* in the far distance. This is the rocky peak at the heart of the city. Its magnificent buildings gleam in the sunlight.

Soon they reach the outskirts of Athens. The busy side streets are full of noisy workshops, and there seems to be lots of people.

Hegeso and Dexileos stare in amazement. Aged ten and eight, they have spent their entire lives in the countryside. They have never experienced anything like the sights, noises and smells of the great city. It's amazing! And rather frightening, too. Hegeso grabs Manes' hand and holds on tightly.

> *"Whoever said that farming is the foundation of all the arts, is quite correct. When all is well on the farms, all is well elsewhere."*
>
> Xenophon in *Oeconomicus*, about 370 BC.

Ι Υ Φ Χ Ψ

Θ Ι Κ Λ Μ Ν Ξ Ο Π Ρ Σ Τ Υ Φ Χ Ψ Ω

The Acropolis of Athens, almost as magnificent today as it was in Hegeso's time.

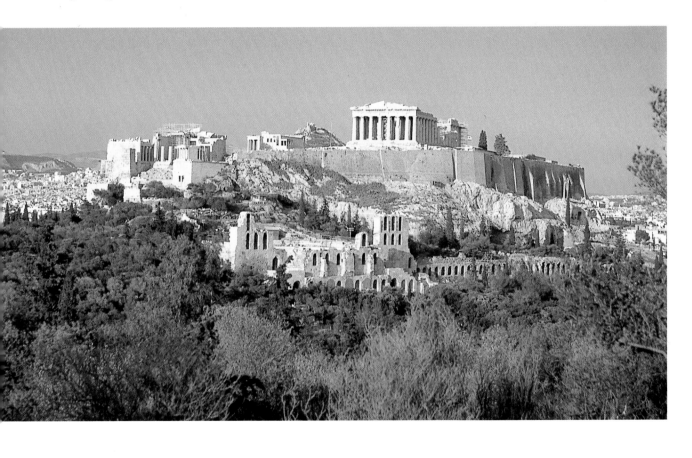

The Agora

Following the Sacred Way, the family passes a huge cemetery and enters the city by a large gate. As they approach the main square called the *Agora*, the street becomes still more crowded with carts and people.

Hegeso thinks the Agora the most fascinating place that she has ever seen. It is surrounded by temples and other fine buildings and jammed with shops, stalls and counters. She follows her father toward the stall of a cheese seller. All of a sudden, she sees a girl about her own age. She smiles. The girl smiles back, then vanishes into the crowd.

A map of ancient Athens. The city was surrounded by high walls and could be entered only through one of the ten gates.

A family visit

The girl Hegeso saw is Lysimache. She and her sister, Praxinoa, live to the north of Athens. Accompanied by four household slaves, Lysimache and Praxinoa are crossing the city with their mother to visit their grandmother. They rarely leave the house and are just as excited as Hegeso and Dexileos by their journey through the city.

"Everyone likes to wander around the city and drop in at the barber's or cobbler's for a chat ... and they always choose somewhere in the Agora rather than a place on the outskirts of the city."

From a speech by Lysias, about 400 BC.

ΘΙΚΛΜΝΞΟΠΡΣΤΥΦΧΨΩ

ΙΥΦΧΨ

Lysimache and Praxinoa live in great comfort. But as is the custom in ancient Greece, they spend most of their time in the *gynaikeion*, the women's quarters on the upper floor of their large house. They see little of their wealthy father. He is always busy with his duties as a citizen.

Across the city

That morning, a slave girl had dressed Lysimache and Praxinoa in their best tunics and given them breakfast. Before leaving, their mother had warned the girls not to speak to anybody and not to stare. Respectable girls, she had insisted, are modest at all times.

Now they are in the street, and the girls are heading toward the Acropolis. Lysimache remembers what her mother told her, but she cannot help looking around at the sights of the wonderful city. She longs to speak with the smiling, simply dressed girl she sees in the Agora but Lysimache knows she should not. Instead, she tries to imagine how different the other girl's life must be.

Lysimache and Praxinoa were wealthy girls rather like the pair in this statuette.

This painted dish shows a shoemaker at his workbench. This was just one of the many kinds of trades that took place in the Agora in ancient Athens.

2 The City and Its People

Hegeso and Lysimache lived in Greece, about 2,450 years ago. Greece was not a true country then, even though the Greeks did think of themselves as a nation. It was divided into a number of small states, each centered on a city. The ancient word for Greece was *Hellas*, and the people living there called themselves *Hellenes*.

The people who eventually called themselves Greeks came into the peninsula from about 2000 BC. By the eighth century BC, they had built up a flourishing civilization. A civilization that lasted until the second century BC, when Greece became part of the Roman Empire. Hegeso and Praxinoa lived during a time that is now called *classical Greece*. Lasting for 150 years, from about 480–330 BC, this was when ancient Greek civilization was at its peak.

Archeologists uncover the remains of Athens' main square, the Agora. Archeology is vitally important in helping us to understand how the ancient Greeks lived.

Ancient glory

We are fascinated by ancient Greece because the roots of much of our government, literature, science and learning go back to that time.

The Greeks have had more influence on our civilization than any other people in history. The very word history comes from the ancient Greek language! Without realizing it, we also use other words that come from the ancient Greek language, such as school and mathematics.

How do we know?

Historians use all sorts of sources to build up a picture of what life was like in ancient Greece. The Greeks were great writers. Although most of their literature has been lost, what remains gives us valuable clues about the way they lived and thought.

Pictures, particularly those on Greek pottery, and other objects discovered by *archeologists* also help us to find out what daily life was like for the ancient Greeks. Buildings and finds, such as weapons, coins and jewelry, help us to form a vision of this wonderful world. Now, after years of research, we have quite a good idea of what it was like to live when Hegeso and Lysimache were alive.

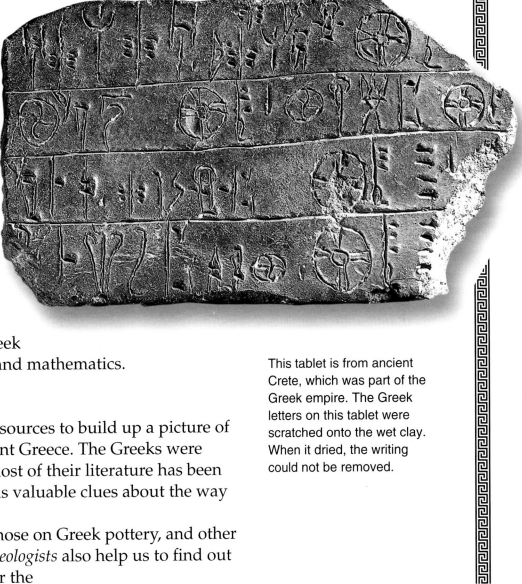

This tablet is from ancient Crete, which was part of the Greek empire. The Greek letters on this tablet were scratched onto the wet clay. When it dried, the writing could not be removed.

"Future ages will wonder at us, as the present age wonders at us now."

The Athenian statesman Pericles in a funeral speech during the Peloponnesian War, 431–404 BC.

Υ
Φ
Χ
Ψ

ΘΙΚΛΜΝΞΟΠΡΣΤΥΦΧΨΩ

The city-states

A city-state in ancient Greece was known as a *polis*, from which we get our word "politics." Most city-states consisted of a walled city and surrounding countryside and agricultural land.

Although all the city-states of ancient Greece shared the same language, and much of the same culture, the way they were governed varied widely. And each state chose its own god as its protector.

Attica

In the classical period, when Hegeso and Lysimache were alive, Attica was by far the wealthiest and most important polis. Its chief city, Athens, was one of the greatest cities of the ancient world.

The world of ancient Greece, showing Attica at its center. The map makes it clear why sea trade was so important to the city of Athens and the territory around it.

Shaped like a triangle, with the sea on two sides, Attica covered about 600 square miles. The area controlled by Attica was actually much larger than this because it had colonies all around the Aegean Sea. In the middle of the fifth century BC, the population of Attica was about 300,000. Because much of its land was of poor agricultural quality, Attica's wealth depended on manufacturing and trade.

> "The skillfully handled Greek ships surrounded the Persians and attacked inward. Many ships turned over, and the sea disappeared beneath blood and wreckage."
>
> Aeschylus, *The Persians*, about 418 BC, describing the Battle of Salamis.

Τ Υ Φ Χ Ψ

Θ Ι Κ Λ Μ Ν Ξ Ο Π Ρ Σ Τ Υ Φ Χ Ψ Ω

Athens

More than a mile across, with the large rocky outcrop (the *Acropolis*) at the center, the city was surrounded by 4 miles of walls. Massive walls also protected the main road to the city's port, Piraeus.

Athens came to dominate Greece after the wars fought against Persia in 490–479 BC. Athens organized the Greek states against the Persian invaders, defeating the enemy at Marathon in 490 BC. Following the Greek naval victory at Salamis (480 BC), Athens entered its "golden age." However, this supremacy did not last long. After the Peloponnesian Wars with Sparta (431-404 BC), Athens never fully recovered its former magnificence.

Fighting between Greek foot soldiers and Persian cavalry on a fifth century Greek vase. The Greeks often fought almost naked.

The government of Athens

During the fifth century BC, Athens, as Attica is often called, developed a system of government known as *democracy*, which means that the government was elected by the people. At a time when all other states and neighboring countries were ruled by a monarchy or by small privileged groups, the Athenians ruled themselves. It was a unique idea and a great source of their strength.

Supreme power rested with the *Assembly*. It met 40 times a year in Athens and was open to all adult male citizens. It business was guided by a Council of 500 citizens, chosen by *lot* from the ten tribes of Attica. Day-to-day decisions were made by the *Prytaneis*, the inner council of 50.

Citizens

Democracy in Attica was not like a modern democracy. Only adult male citizens had a say in the government. A citizen was someone born of a marriage between two citizens. Very occasionally, outsiders could be made citizens by special decree. Otherwise, the citizen body remained a fixed and privileged few.

Citizens of Athens casting their votes at an election. Women, slaves and foreigners were not permitted to become citizens, so power rested in the hands of a small minority of residents.

Women, men under the age of 18, foreigners living in Athens (known as *metics*) and slaves were excluded. This meant that, although the total population of Attica was perhaps 300,000, only about 45,000 could attend the Assembly.

Demes

All citizens belonged to a complicated network of groups. As well as their family, they were part of a kind of brotherhood, known as a *phratry*. They were also members of religious, dining and sporting organizations.

For administration, Attica was divided up into *phylai*, *trittyes* and *demes*. There were ten phylai, each consisting of three trittyes – one city area, one coastal area and one inland area. The 170 demes were the smallest units. Each one was supervised by a *demarchos* who was elected by the citizens of that deme for one year.

"We call our system of government a democracy because power rests with everyone, not with a tiny minority."

Pericles' funeral speech, delivered in the winter of 431–430 BC.

ΟΠΡΣΤΥΦΧΨ

ΠΡΣΤΥΦΧΨΩ

Metics

Metics were the 50,000 foreigners living in Attica. They played no part in the government and paid only light taxes. They were also free to own slaves.

Most metics were businessmen or craftsmen such as metalworkers and weavers. A few were teachers or doctors. The Athenians realized that metics were valuable members of the community, and the punishment for murdering a metic was death.

Slavery

Slavery was an accepted part of Athenian life. Over half the population of Attica was made up of slaves. They did mostly manual work, giving citizens time for their duties, their work and their leisure.

Slaves were seen as objects. They were prisoners of war or kidnap victims and could be bought in the Agora slave market for between 150 and 300 *drachmas* (at that time, a soldier or craftsman received about 1 drachma a day). Most slaves received no pay. Their children belonged to their master, and runaway slaves were branded with a red-hot iron.

A woman and her maid. Serving girls were slaves. They received no wages and had to do precisely as they were told.

In Attica, the slaves' lives gradually improved. They were protected against unnecessary cruelty, and toward the end of the classical period, some thinkers were even suggesting that slavery itself might be wrong.

Slaves' work

Most citizens owned slaves. Hegeso's father had two who helped in the house and three farm slaves. Lysimache's father was much wealthier, and had a dozen slaves doing the housework under a slave master, who was himself a slave. The most important slaves were the doorkeeper, gardener, cooks, secretary and maids.

The state owned slaves, too. Slave clerks and minor officials were paid a salary and allowed to marry. The best-known state slaves were the 1,000 Scythian archers employed as Athens' police force. Life was hardest for slave grain grinders and miners in the silver mines. The miners worked in terrible conditions, and punishments for disobedience were severe. The death rate among them was very high.

"The human race has certain inferior individuals ...
.Nature has destined such people to become slaves, for they are ideally suited to obeying."
Aristotle, *Politics*, about 340 BC.

Τ Υ Φ Χ Ψ

Ə Ι Κ Λ Μ Ν Ξ Ο Π Ρ Σ Τ Υ Φ Χ Ψ Ω

Slaves hurrying to a banquet with food for the guests.

3 At Home and School

The city of Athens has been rebuilt many times since the classical period, and the remains of the ancient city lie well below the present street level. This means that we only have an idea of what a house was like. The houses excavated by archeologists are small and simple, so we can only guess what larger houses, such as Lysimache's wealthy father's house, would have been like.

It was probably two stories high, with flat roofs. Bigger houses were probably built around a courtyard. The women's quarters were probably on the upper floor. There was a kitchen and bathroom, but the fire used for cooking was lit outside and brought indoors when needed. We also know that the walls were thin, because there are reports of robbers digging through the walls of the house!

An artist's impression of what a large Greek house might have looked like. Only the best houses were built around a courtyard.

Kitchen

Bedroom

Andron (where men entertain guests)

Courtyard

Gynaikeion (womens quarters)

Workroom

Entrance

Country houses

As far as we can tell, farmhouses and other houses in the country were quite small. This means that Hegeso's house was probably only one story high. The rooms were probably arranged around a courtyard, which had a well in the center.

As in the town, the women's and men's rooms were probably separate. The kitchen and bathroom may have been next to each other, so that the bathroom was kept warm in the winter. Chamber pots were used instead of lavatories, and there was no running water. The walls were most likely plain plaster, with nails or wooden pegs for hanging things on.

Furniture and equipment

Greek houses were much less cluttered than modern houses. Furniture was simple and consisted of beds and couches, chairs and stools, lamps, chests for storage and three-legged tables.

Cooking was done on an open fire, using metal pots. Food was served on wooden plates, but without forks or spoons. Earthenware jars of many shapes and designs were used for storing food and drink.

This beautiful bronze vessel, probably a charcoal burner, was made in the fourth century BC. Bronze, a mixture of copper and tin, was widely used in ancient Greece because it is tough but easy to work and does not rust.

"Let me tell you ...that my tiny house has an upper story. The rooms are arranged the same upstairs and downstairs, with the women's quarters on one floor and the men's on the other."
Lysias, *On the Murder of Eratosthenes*, about 400 BC.

ΘΙΚΛΜΝΞΟΠΡΣΤΥΦΧΨΩ

ΤΥΦΧΨ

Families

Athens was a man's world. Men ran the city-state and organized everything to suit themselves. Families were very important to the ancient Greeks, but their idea of a family was quite different from ours.

The father was the head of the family, and everyone had to do as he said. In some families, the men did not see much of the women. Wives stayed at home and ran the household. A husband could divorce his wife if she was unfaithful or if they had no children. It was much more difficult for a wife to divorce her husband.

A Greek bride washing at an indoor fountain as she prepares for her wedding.

Marriage

Marriages were arranged by fathers, close male relatives or guardians. They were not romantic unions between two people who had fallen in love. Love might grow between a married couple, but the main purpose of a marriage was to produce children to continue the family name and honor their parents after they had died.

The marriage ceremony was in two parts. First came the betrothal, or engagement. This was an agreement that the marriage would take place. The bride-to-be may not even have been present. Weddings often took place in the winter on the day of a full moon. The central part of the ceremony was a procession taking the bride to her husband's house.

Women

Compared with women today, women in classical Attica lived very restricted lives. Respectable young women rarely left their women's quarters, known as the *gynaikeion*. Lysimache's mother went out occasionally to attend a festival. Otherwise, she would have stayed at home with the keys of the house at her waist as a symbol of her authority.

Women from poorer families, especially in the country, enjoyed greater freedom. When one of their slaves was ill, Hegeso's mother would probably have helped with farm work. The least restricted women were the wives of metics.

A mother and her child. The woman is wearing the baggy tunic known as a *peplos.* Like all respectable Greek women, she has her head covered.

A betrothal scene from Menander's play *Periceiromene.* Pataecus is the person legally responsible for the girl he is giving away. Polemon is the suitor.

PATAECUS I give you this girl so that she may produce children in marriage.

POLEMON I accept her.

PATAECUS I agree to provide her with a dowry of three talents.

POLEMON I accept that as well. Thank you.

Σ Τ Υ Φ Χ Ψ

ΑΒΓΔΕΖΗΘΙΚΛΜΝΞΟΠΡΣΤΥΦΧΨΩ

A new baby

Before a baby was born, the house was daubed with pitch to ward off evil spirits. The birth was attended by several women, some of whom were midwives. After the birth, an olive branch was hung outside the house if the child was a boy, and a strip of woolen cloth for a girl. A special ceremony was held about a week later. Three days after that, the parents made a sacrifice to the gods and named the child.

Citizens did not generally have big families. A wife could have an abortion, with her husband's consent. Citizens would also rid themselves of an unwanted baby by placing it in a clay pot, which also acted as its tomb, and leaving it to die.

The ancient Greeks' attitude toward childbirth was practical rather than romantic. This early sixth- century tablet reads, "Hermon wants to know to which god he should pray for his wife to bear useful children."

Children

Boys were in the care of their mothers until they went to school. Girls remained with their mothers until they left home to get married. Newborn babies were wrapped in tight *swaddling clothes* and breast-fed by their mothers. They often slept in wicker cradles and were entertained with lullabies.

Boys seem to have worn few clothes about the house. Girls dressed in simple tunics. Many children are pictured wearing a string of charms to ward off bad luck and illness.

Toys and games

Like many ancient Greek children, Hegeso and Dexileos had all sorts of toys to play with when they were young. Hegeso and Dexileos' father made them rattles and a tiny chariot that could be pulled along on a piece of string. They also liked the animal figures and dolls that Manes the slave made for them.

When they were older, they played ball outside the house. Sometimes, when they were bored, they took their pet weasel, Pipos, into the barn and watched him catch mice!

"Sleep, O my children, sleep in peace and calm.
Brother with brother, sleep my lovely boys,
Blessed in both your slumbers and your waking."

A lullaby by the poet Theocritus, about 280 BC.

Τ
Υ
Φ
Χ
Ψ

Θ Ι Κ Λ Μ Ν Ξ Ο Π Ρ Σ Τ Υ Φ Χ Ψ Ω

A child's doll made of pottery. The arms and legs are held on with pins so they can move.

To school

In Athens, citizens could only attend private schools that charged fees. The city paid for boys whose fathers had died for their country. As there were no girls' schools, girls had to learn what they could from their mothers or from an educated slave.

Boys were taught at home until the age of seven. Then, if there was a school nearby, they went to daily classes. Each pupil was accompanied by his *paedagogos*. This was a household slave who watched over the boy's progress and punished him if he was lazy or misbehaved. Pupils sat on stools before the teacher, each with his paedagogos watching in the background. The school day lasted from dawn to dusk, with no weekends off or school holidays. The only breaks from lessons were during festivals.

A girl reading from a scroll. There were no girls' schools in ancient Greece, so girls had to pick up what education they could from their mothers or from slaves.

Writing

A schoolboy's main equipment consisted of a wooden board, covered in wax and a stylus. This was a sharp rod, like a pen, for writing on the wax. When they were older, they wrote on a kind of paper known as *papyrus*. Ink came in solid blocks that had to be mixed with water before it could be used.

"If a child obeys his teachers, that's fine. If he doesn't, he is brought into shape with threats and blows, like a piece of wood that is bent or warped."

Plato, recording the words of Protagoras, fifth century BC.

ΘΙΚΛΜΝΞΟΠΡΣΤΥΦΧΨΩ

Subjects

The first two or three years were spent learning to read and write. Pupils then moved on to learning passages by heart, especially the works of the famous Greek poet Homer. Mathematics was very difficult because the Greeks used the letters of the alphabet for numbers but had no way of writing zero.

Music and sport were also important to the ancient Greeks. They considered music the foundation of all culture - the very word *music* comes from the Muses, the Greek goddesses who guided all arts and learning. Pupils learned to play the *aulos*, a kind of flute, and the *kithara*, a lyre. Physical education began at the age of 12 with boxing and athletics.

Learning to play the kithara, or lyre. Music was an essential part of a Greek boy's education.

4 Daily Life

Everything the Greeks made came from natural substances. They used stone, clay and marble for building, iron, tin and copper for tools and weapons, and wool, leather, linen, cotton and silk for clothing. Synthetic substances, such as plastics and nylon, were unknown. Cotton and silk were luxuries.

Male dress

Greek men were quite used to being seen with no clothes on. They met together, naked, in the public baths, and most athletes competed in the nude.

The basic item of male dress was the woolen tunic, either the everyday *exomis*, draped over one shoulder, or the *chiton*, worn on both shoulders and gathered in folds about the waist. Both were tied round the waist with a girdle.

In cold weather, men wore a large rectangle of wool, known as a *himation*, which was carefully draped over the left shoulder. They went barefoot indoors but put on leather sandals when going out. Most men had beards and quite short hair.

Two golden rings. The snake ring may have been worn to bring good health, because the snake was a symbol of healing.

"Isomachus noticed that his wife was wearing make-up. She had white lead on her face, to make it even whiter, and red juice on her cheeks. She was in high-heels, too!"

From Xenophon's *Oeconomicus*, about 380 BC.

ΑΒΓΔΕΖΗΘΙΚΛΜΝΞΟΠΡΣΤΥΦΧΨΩ

Female dress

Women's clothing was also based on a large rectangle of wool or linen. This was made into a *peplos*. This was a type of open tunic which could be pinned on each shoulder or sewn up to make a dress. A large peplos could be pulled over the head and worn like a hood. It could also be worn with or without a girdle.

Like men, women wore sandals outdoors, and in cold weather women wore shawls. Wealthy women often carried parasols to keep off the sun and rain.

At the time of the Persian wars, both men and women wore jewelry. In classical times, men wore only a signet ring. Women had a wide choice of necklaces, bracelets, earrings and anklets, made of precious metal, amber, jade or ivory. They wore eye-liner, face make-up and often dyed their hair.

A statue of the goddess Kore, also known as Persephone. The way she wears her peplos in elegant folds was typical of wealthy Greek women.

Meal times

The Greeks took their main meal between five and six o'clock in the evening.

Because the ancient Greeks had no accurate way of telling the time, they organized their days by the sun. The hours of daylight were divided into early morning, late morning, afternoon and evening. Appointments and meal times were often arranged according to the length of a shadow cast by a long stick, a time stick.

By the time the ancient Greeks ate their main meal, the shadow from a time stick might be between six and twenty feet long.

A *symposion*, or drinking party. The guests were all men, although slave girls sometimes served the food, played music and danced for their entertainment.

The Symposion

The best-known Greek meal was the *symposion,* literally meaning "drinking party." The modern equivalent would be a dinner party. It was held in a private house, and only male guests were invited. They sat or lay on couches and had food and drink brought to them by slaves.

The symposion began with the meal and continued with drinking and entertainment. Fashionable dinners sometimes included delicacies such as roasted songbird, snails, fish roe (eggs), tuna and even grasshoppers. After dinner the guests told stories and held discussions, recited poetry and enjoyed the music and dancing of slave girls.

"I am not keen to hear the man who drinks his wine
And talks of serious things like war all the time."

From the poet Anacreon, mid-sixth century BC.

I
Υ
Φ
Χ
Ψ

Η Θ Ι Κ Λ Μ Ν Ξ Ο Π Ρ Σ Τ Υ Φ Χ Ψ Ω

Food and drink

Most Greeks ate a healthy and well-balanced diet. Their main food was bread, with which they would eat green vegetables, beans, lentils, eggs, cheese, garlic, olives and olive oil.

Meat was expensive and rarely eaten, but fish was plentiful and a rich source of protein for the ancient Greeks. Meals were flavored with herbs and aniseed.

The ancient Greeks enjoyed their fruit, too, and figs and grapes grew well on their hillsides. Sweet dishes were often made with delicious honey.

Breakfast and lunch were light meals, consisting of bread, wine and perhaps cheese or olives. The evening meal was fuller and often accompanied by quantities of wine. Water, goat's milk and wine were drunk from pottery cups. Wine was served from leather bottles and stored in clay jars known as *pithoi.*

Keeping clean

The Greeks were keen on personal hygiene. Women washed at home, from a bowl or stone fountain, while men liked to meet in public baths. The favorite bath time was in the hour before the evening meal. Public baths and swimming pools, with their steam rooms and cold plunge pools, became popular meeting places.

Soap was unknown to the ancient Greeks. Instead they washed with a special kind of clay and other rough substances. Afterward, they liked to rub oil over their bodies and have it scraped off by a slave, leaving the skin clean and tingling.

Keeping fit

Most ancient Greek men liked to keep themselves in good shape. Even old men exercised to keep themselves fit. The Greeks made frequent use of the *gymnasion*. The ancient Greeks admired and respected people with physical strength, so visits to the gymnasion were as much about boosting their social standing as making themselves attractive.

Lysimache's father exercised in the *palaestra*. This was a large, square, open-air sports ground, with changing rooms and bathhouses around the edge.

There were regular sports events all over Greece, the most famous of which were the Olympic Games. A returning champion was greeted as a hero and rewarded with feasts, honors and presents.

Women washing at home. Public bathhouses were for men only.

"That little monkey Cleigenes, the most wicked bath attendant who ever lived!"
From Aristophanes' play *Frogs*, about 410 BC.

Υ Φ Χ Ψ

ΘΙΚΛΜΝΞΟΠΡΣΤΥΦΧΨΩ

Sports and games

Sporting festivals in ancient Greece involved all kinds of events. There were running races over various distances, horse races, long-jump and discus-throwing competitions, boxing and wrestling matches – and sometimes even a race when the competitors dressed in armor!

Other outdoor pursuits included fishing, hunting and various ball games. The Greeks loved gambling and bet on horse races and cock fights or on simple games with dice.

Greek boxers with their hands bound with oxhide. As a fight did not take place in a ring and could last for hours, broken bones were common.

Religion

The ancient Greeks believed in many gods and goddesses. They thought the gods were rather like superhumans who controlled everything from the growing of crops to victory in war and the success of a marriage. Religion was therefore tremendously important, touching all aspects of everyday life.

Zeus was king of the gods, and he lived on Mount Olympus. Many ancient Greeks had an altar to Zeus in their homes.

Worship

Greek worship involved prayer, sacrifice and purification. Prayers usually meant asking the gods for something or praising them. Prayers were made either standing up with the arms outstretched, or lying face down on the ground.

Because the gods and goddesses were thought to be rather like humans, they were offered things that humans valued. These might be animals, such as sheep, oxen or deer, which were sacrificed and burned. Other offerings included honey cakes and grain. Purification was the cleansing of body and soul that took place at various special ceremonies.

Temples and festivals

The ancient Greeks honored their deities with hundreds of temples and statues. The temples were usually very grand buildings, with roofs supported by rows of spectacular columns. The most famous statue of the goddess Athena stood on the Acropolis. Made of gold and ivory, it stood almost thirty feet high.

There was a whole range of religious festivals. Three of the largest in Athens were:
• the Eleusinian Mysteries, held at the end of the summer in honor of Demeter, the goddess of crops, and her daughter Persephone.

A bronze statue of the god Zeus about to throw a thunderbolt. Zeus was also known as the the god of sky and thunder.

Awesome even today, the temple of Athena on the acropolis of Lindos on the isle of Rhodes.

• the Great Panathenaia which was held every four years near the middle of the summer in honor of Athena, the goddess of wisdom, art and war.
• the City Dionysia, a spring festival held for Dionysus, the god of the grapevine, which incorporated drama.

Oracles

An *oracle* was a place where Greeks could ask their deities for advice. The most famous oracle was at the city of Delphi, where priests of Apollo answered questions.Their predictions were carefully worded, so that they would be right whatever happened!

An ancient Greek prayer:

"If I have honored you with burnt sacrifices of the heavy thighs of bulls and goats, answer my prayer."

Υ
Φ
Χ
Ψ

ΘΙΚΛΜΝΞΟΠΡΣΤΥΦΧΨΩ

Medicine

Greek medicine was a mixture of folk remedies, superstition and science. Men and women had always noticed the healing effects of certain plants and herbs, and doctors used them for healing the sick. But just as important were prayers, offerings and sacrifices to Asclepius, the god of healing.

There were all sorts of doctors in Athens, but the most reliable had been trained on the island of Cos, which boasted the best medical school in the region. Led by Hippocrates, the founder of the school, these doctors tried to find out how the body worked. They then tried to identify the different kinds of diseases and medicines to cure them.

Death and burial

In Greek mythology, the dead crossed the River Styx to the Underworld. This was the kingdom of Hades. Because the ancient Greeks believed in this passage to another world, a funeral and its preparations were very important.

The body was perfumed with oils and laid out at home in clean clothes, with a garland of flowers round the head. A coin was sometimes put in the mouth to pay the Styx ferryman. The dead person's most valued possessions were also placed in the coffin. Family members shaved their heads and wore mourning clothes. Then there was much ritual weeping and wailing.

Thanks, Asclepius! This plaque was made to thank Asclepius, the god of healing, for making a patient's leg better.

Part of the oath sworn by new doctors in ancient Greece. It is said to have been devised by Hippocrates.

"I swear by Apollo ... that whatever house I enter, I will do so only to help the sick ..."

This gold crown of ivy leaves was found in a tomb from the fourth century BC. People were often buried with their treasured possessions.

The cult of the dead

Funerals took place at night, when dead bodies were taken beyond the city walls to be buried or burned. Slaves were laid in the same family tomb as their masters. These tombs were marked with marble slabs, some rather grand and elaborately carved.

Children were expected to honor their dead relatives, particularly their fathers. People would often make offerings to a small statue of their dead father. This ensured the well-being of the deceased in the next world.

Laying out a dead body. This painting shows mourners preparing a body for a funeral.

The law

The people of Athens had great respect for the law. They believed it was what held the city together. To break the law was to go against the will of the citizens, because their will was the law.

The law was upheld by individuals and by the police force of archers known as the Scythian archers. It was controlled by "the Eleven," which was a group of magistrates. The state could not prosecute anyone. A person accused of a crime, even a crime against Athens itself, had to be taken to court by another individual.

Soldiers like this Scythian archer made up the Athenian police force.

Courts

The Athenian system of law courts was extremely complicated. The courts were supervised by magistrates who were citizens. The decision about whether someone was guilty or not was made by a *jury* of fellow citizens. The jury might contain as many as 2001 men! Really serious cases about the security of Athens might be heard by the whole Assembly.

In court, the person bringing the case known as the plaintiff and the accused both presented their cases. They could employ professionals to write their speeches for them. The jury was not allowed to interrupt, although it might let its feelings be known by murmuring. When both sides had finished, the jury voted on whether the accused was guilty or not. There was always an odd number of people on the jury, so there was always a majority vote.

Names of the banned. The citizens of Athens could vote to have someone ostracized (sent away from the city for 10 years) by writing their name on a piece of pottery. You can clearly see the name Aristeides, who was ostracized in 482 BC.

Punishment

Punishments varied widely. There were different punishments for citizens, metics and slaves. Those who confessed to a murder did not even get to court, they were executed on the spot. Those found guilty of murder in a trial were hung by the hands, wrists and feet outside the city walls, and left to die.

Other punishments included fines, confiscation of property, banishment and, rarely, imprisonment. Only slaves might be whipped and branded.

"I will vote according to the laws and decrees of the Assembly and Council. Where there are no laws, I will find the most just answer, without showing any favors ..."

Part of the oath probably sworn by Athenian jurors.

ΑΒΓΔΕΖΗΘΙΚΛΜΝΞΟΠΡΣΤΥΦΧΨΩ

5 Work and Duty

The power and wealth of Athens depended on the city's businesses. Many citizens had jobs, but they felt no disgrace in increasing their wealth through trade. Lysimache's father made money by importing grain from Scythia, to the north of the Black Sea. He did not need to have a job and would have felt it was beneath him to work for a wage. Wages, citizens believed, took away their freedom. The ideal life was said to be that of the independent small farmer.

A Greek merchant ship about 540 BC. Ships like these traded all over the Mediterranean and were the key to Athens' wealth and power.

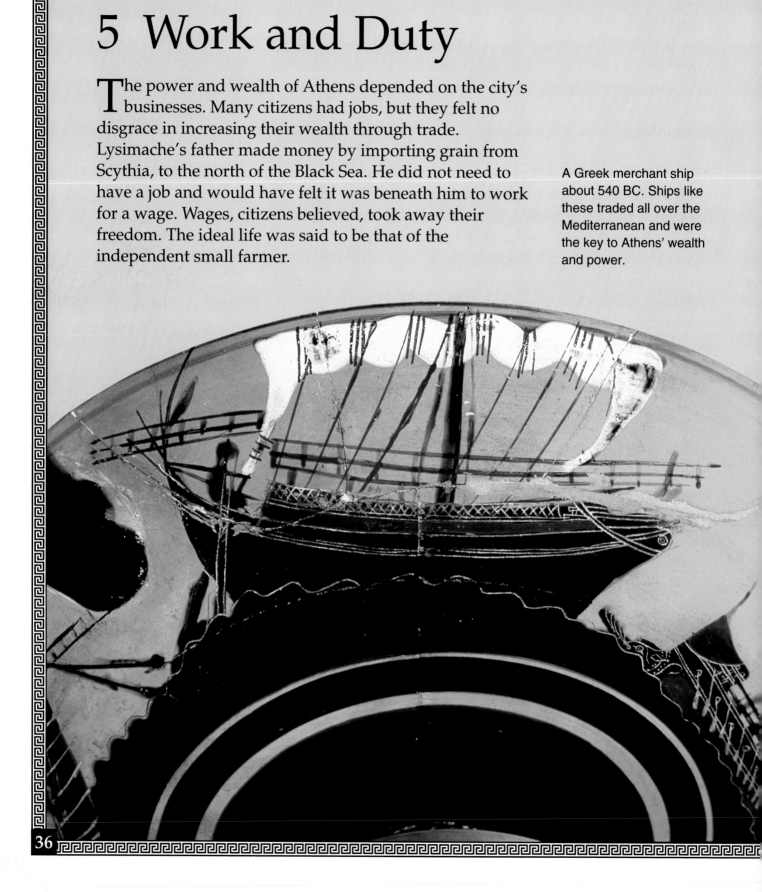

Athens' wealth owed a great deal to its *colonies*. Founded by Athenians all over the eastern Mediterranean, the colonies provided raw materials such as timber and grain. In 483 BC, the discovery of vast stocks of silver at Maronea in Thrace added greatly to Athens' prosperity.

Merchants and traders

The port of Piraeus was one of the busiest in the Mediterranean. Trading ships came laden with grain, raw materials and luxuries. They left with wine and products from the city's many workshops.

One of the largest workshops was owned by the metic Cephalus, who employed 120 slaves in the manufacture of weapons and armor. Most other businesses were much smaller and included potteries and cloth workshops, shops, taverns and market stalls.

Money

Silver from Laurium and Maronea enabled Athens to *mint* many different coins. These included a coin with the goddess Athena's head on one side and an owl, the moon and an olive branch on the other.

The basic coin was the silver *drachma*. There were two- and ten-drachma coins, too. The *mina* (100 drachma) and the *talent* (6000 drachma) were used for counting but never made into coins. Small amounts were paid for in *obols*. An obol was one-sixth of a drachma. The tiniest coin was worth one quarter of an obol.

A silver tetradrachma (four drachma) coin from the region of Boeotia.

"It is impossible to be a proper citizen if one does manual labor for wages."

From Aristotle's *Politics*, middle of the fourth century BC.

Φ
Χ
Ψ

ΘΙΚΛΜΝΞΟΠΡΣΤΥΦΧΨΩ

Agriculture

Hegeso's father was typical of the sturdy farmer regarded as the backbone of Attica. From his own land he produced enough for himself, his family and his slaves. He sold surplus produce in the Agora, using the money to buy goods that could not be made on the farm.

Hegeso and her family were lucky to live during prosperous times for farmers. In the previous century, most of Attica had been owned by a few wealthy landlords. Later, during the Peloponnesian Wars, some farms were ravaged by invading armies. They destroyed the vines and olive trees and ruined agriculture in the area for many years to come.

On the farm

Farmers on hilly ground kept sheep, goats and pigs. The milk from goats and ewes was made into cheese. There were not many cattle in Attica because the quality of the grass was poor.

Grain and vegetables were grown in the valleys and on the plains. Farmers tilled the soil three times a year, using a plow pulled by a mule. The grain was cut by hand and threshed by animals trampling over it. Slaves then ground the grain into flour. Some farmers also collected honey to sell in the city.

Rows of olive trees in modern Greece. In ancient times, olives were associated with the goddess Athena and provided fuel and food.

"As I gaze toward the countryside, I long for peace. I'm sick of the town and miss my old village, where no one ever talked of buying and selling ..."

From the play *Acharnians* by Aristophanes, about 400 BC.

Τ
Υ
Φ
Χ
Ψ

Θ Ι Κ Λ Μ Ν Ξ Ο Π Ρ Σ Τ Υ Φ Χ Ψ Ω

Worshipers offer sacrifices to Demeter, the goddess of agriculture or "mother earth." Ancient Greeks believed that she would help their crops to grow if they pleased her with their gifts.

Vines and olives

Vines and olives were the most valuable crops. They grew best on sunny hillsides. Grapes from the vines were crushed and the juice turned into wine. Water was usually added before the wine was drunk. The ancient Greeks thought it *barbaric* not to dilute, and the mixing of wine and water at the symposion became a symbol for balance and moderate behavior in social life.

The oil from olives had all sorts of uses. It was used in cookery, as it is today. It was also burned as a fuel, rubbed on the body and turned into cosmetics. According to legend, Athena and Poseidon, the god of horses and the sea, once competed for Attica. Poseidon produced the horse, Athena the olive. Since the olive was thought more useful, Athena won and Athens was named after her.

The duties of a citizen

Athens was run by its adult male citizens. They spent a great deal of time on their civic duties. For Lysimache's father, this was hardly a problem, because he lived in Athens and needed only a few hours each week for his own business.

Hegeso's father found the duties of citizenship more difficult. He attended the Assembly whenever he could and tried to get to meetings of his deme. Occasionally, he served on a jury, and sometimes he served as a city official.

Military service

Until the fourth century BC, Athens relied on its citizens to make up her armed forces. This meant that all men had to train and keep fit. When they were 18, they began two years' military training. For the next 40 years, they had to be prepared to do *military service* at any time.

A man's service depended on how much property he owned. The wealthy joined the cavalry, because maintaining a horse was a costly business. The less well-off went into either the heavy or the light *infantry*. Those with least property served in the navy.

A Greek foot soldier, or *"hoplite,"* ready for action. The long spear was useful against cavalry attack.

A modern reconstruction of a Greek *trireme*, a warship that was powered by human rowers.

The navy

In the fifth century BC, Athens wanted to control the whole of Greece. To do this, it needed a large army and a powerful navy. The navy was essential to protect its traders and colonies and to resist invaders. By this time, Athens also used foreign mercenaries and allied troops.

The navy was first built up by Themistocles. He persuaded the citizens to use Athens' silver to construct a fleet of some 200 ships, which he led in the great victory at Salamis. As the navy grew in size, poorer citizens had the opportunity to become more imporant.

"I shall bring no dishonor to the sacred arms I carry; I shall never desert my fellow soldiers; I shall fight to defend my land and its holy places ..."

From the oath sworn by all Athenians beginning military training.

Τ
Υ
Φ
Χ
Ψ

ΘΙΚΛΜΝΞΟΠΡΣΤΥΦΧΨΩ

6 The Greek Legacy

An obvious *legacy* from the ancient Greek language is the many words we still use every day. These include *character, music, gymnasium, magic,* and *drama.* Some common prefixes (such as *poly* -) and suffixes (such as *-ology*) also come from the ancient Greek language, too.

The Greek alphabet, which begins alpha (α), beta (β), gamma (γ) is the basis of our own alphabet. And where do you think we get the word *alphabet* from?

Literature and ideas

For centuries, Greek civilization was the best in the Western world. It was spread east and west by traders, travelers and warriors, such as the mighty leader Alexander the Great (356–323 BC) of Macedonia in northern Greece. Even when Greece was swallowed up by the Roman Empire, many still regarded Greek as the language of scholarship.

"Nobody can say a word against Greek: it stamps a man at once as an educated gentleman."

The Irish playwright George Bernard Shaw in *Major Barbara*, 1907.

Υ Φ Χ Ψ

ΘΙΚΛΜΝΞΟΠΡΣΤΥΦΧΨΩ

Long after ancient Greece and Rome had fallen, knowledge of Greek was thought of as essential for a good education. Generation after generation of schoolchildren were brought up knowing almost as much of Homer, Plato and Aristotle as they did of English writers such as Chaucer and Shakespeare. This affected the way they wrote, spoke and thought.

Science and mathematics

Many of ancient Greece's finest mathematicians, philosophers and scientists flourished outside the Greek mainland.

The philosopher Pythagoras (sixth century BC) settled in southern Italy. Hippocrates the doctor lived on the island of Cos in about 469–399 BC. Plato and Aristotle, the fourth-century BC philosophers, taught in Athens but traveled widely around the Greek-speaking world. For a time, Aristotle taught Alexander the Great. The mathematician and scientist Archimedes came from Syracuse in Sicily and trained in Alexandria.

The ideas and teachings of all these men, and many more like them, are still widely read and admired. They still form a part in the development of our own civilization today.

An artist's idea of what the Greek poet Homer may have looked like.

Architecture

The Greeks devised a distinctive style of building. It was so impressive that it has been copied and adapted by many different cultures.

After the collapse of the Roman Empire in the fifth century AD, the classical style of architecture was not widely used for several centuries. It reappeared at the time of the *Renaissance*, which began in the fourteenth century and continued to the end of the sixteenth century. Classical architecture has since emerged in most European and American countries.

Art

The branches of Greek art that we find most remarkable are pottery and sculpture. Athenian vases, which came in five basic shapes, were the finest in the Mediterranean area. Not only were they made in graceful designs, but they were skillfully painted. In the sixth century BC, the pattern was black drawing on a red or orange background. In the following century this changed to red designs on a black background. Future generations of potters, such as the English firm Wedgwood in the nineteenth century, have been heavily influenced by Athenian skill.

Like Greek architecture, Greek sculpture was "rediscovered" at the time of the Renaissance. The lifelike work of Greek sculptors in stone and bronze inspired Renaissance masters like Michelangelo and Cellini.

The influence of Greek architecture can be clearly seen in the design of the Capitol Building in Washington, DC. It was built between 1851 and 1863.

The Birth of Venus, by the Italian Renaissance painter Sandro Botticelli (1445–1510). Venus was the Roman name for Aphrodite, the Greek goddess of love.

The Greek spirit

Perhaps the greatest gift the Greeks gave to the world was a belief in the worth of the individual human being. Although they did not extend this respect to slaves and women, they set out a framework of thinking that later cultures extended to all humankind.

Our respect for democracy, the law and human rights stems directly from the achievements of the Athenians of the fifth century BC. This perhaps helps to explain our fascination with a civilization that lived so long ago.

Items of pottery from the firm founded by the English businessman Josiah Wedgwood in the 1760s. He employed the best artists to copy classical designs from ancient Greece and Rome.

> *"The mountains look on Marathon -*
> *And Marathon looks on the sea;*
> *And musing there an hour alone,*
> *I dreamed that Greece might still be free."*

From *Don Juan* by Lord Byron, the English poet who died fighting for Greek independence in 1824.

Τ
Υ
Φ
Χ
Ψ

ΘΙΚΛΜΝΞΟΠΡΣΤΥΦΧΨΩ

Glossary

Acropolis
A fortress. The most famous is the Acropolis of Athens.

Agora
The marketplace in the center of Athens.

Archeologist
A person who studies history by discovering old buildings and objects found buried in the ground.

Assembly
A group of specially selected people who had the right to speak and vote on important state matters.

Aulos
A musical instrument that was a cross between a flute and an oboe, although it is usually translated as a flute.

Barbaric
Rough and sometimes cruel behavior.

Classical Greece
500-336 BC, the period after the Archaic Period and before the Hellenistic Age.

Colonies
Countries settled by people from a different country.

Democracy
Government by the people. In Athens this meant by the male citizens.

Drachma
A silver Athenian coin weighing 4.36 grams.

Gymnasion
A room or building with equipment and space to exercise and keep fit.

Infantry
A group of soldiers who march and fight on foot.

Jury
The people who hear both sides of a case in court and decide whether the accused person is guilty or not.

Kithara
A lyre. Originally it had six strings, but this increased to seven or eight later.

Legacy
A way of thinking or a possession passed down from one generation to another.

Linen
Cloth made from the flax plant.

Lot
Make a decision by drawing a name (or lot) from a selection of names put forward.

Lyre
A stringed musical instrument rather like a guitar.

Magistrate
An official responsible for upholding the law.

Metic
A foreigner resident in Athens.

Military Service
A period of time that people voluntarily or involuntarily spend with one of the armed forces (navy, army or airforce).

Minoan
The civilization that thrived on Crete from 2000–1450 BC

Mint
A place where coins are made.

Mythology
Stories and legends.

Oracle
A place where people could consult a god or goddess through special priests or priestesses.

Papyrus
A type of paper made from reeds

Pericles
Athenian statesman and general who dominated Athens about 460-431 BC.

Philosopher
A person who uses reason and deep thought to understand and make sense of human life.

Piraeus
The port of Athens.

Pithoi
Storage jars made from clay.

Polis
A city-state and its people.

Poseidon
God of earthquakes and the sea.

Prosecute
To take legal action against somebody you believe has broken the law.

Pythagoras
Sixth-century BC philosopher and mathematician.

Renaissance
A revival of art and architecture from the classical period, in the fourteenth century AD.

Sacrifice
To kill an animal as an offering to a god or goddess.

Styx
The boundary river of the Underworld across which the dead passed by ferry.

Swaddling clothes
Thin strips of cloth wrapped around a baby.

Trireme
An ancient Greek warship with three rows of oars on each side.

Underworld
The place where people went when they died. Sometimes known as Hades.

Time line

All dates are BC

c. 1200	The Dorian people, the last invaders from the north, come to Greece
c. 1100	First Greek colonies on the coast of Asia Minor
c. 776	First recorded Olympic Games
c. 750	Greek colonies in Italy
c. 750–700	Homer composing the Iliad and the Odyssey
c. 705	Greeks begin building in stone
c. 700	Attica formed
c. 683	Athens becomes a republic
c. 650	Classic Greek sculpture appears
c. 600	Black-figure vase painting appears
c. 594	Athens' constitution reformed by Solon
c. 525	Red-figure vase painting appears
c. 508	Democratic reforms in Athens
490–479	Persian Wars
490	Battle of Marathon - Greeks defeat the Persian invaders
483	New supply of silver found at Laurium
480	Battle of Salamis - Greeks defeat the Persian fleet
c. 480	Playwright Euripides born
c. 469	Hippocrates the famous doctor born
462–1 (to 431)	Democratic reforms of Pericles in Athens. The "golden age" of Athens sees the building of the Parthenon and other fine buildings.
c. 460	Historian Thucydides born
457	Long Walls built between Athens and Piraeus
c. 454	Athens dominates most of Greece
c. 450	Playwright Aristophanes born
431–404	Peloponnesian War between Athens and Sparta
427	Philosopher Plato born
404	Athens surrenders to Sparta
384	Philosopher Aristotle born
336–323	Reign of Alexander the Great of Macedonia
c. 287	Archimedes born
147	Macedonia becomes part of Roman Empire
146	All of Greece absorbed into the Roman Empire

Further Information

Books for children:

THE ATLAS OF THE CLASSICAL WORLD
by Piero Bardi, Peter Bedrick Books 1997
ANCIENT GREECE
by John D. Clare, ed., Harcourt Brace 1994
ANCIENT GREEKS AT A GLANCE
by John Malam, Peter Bedrick Books 1998
GREECE (Ancient World series)
by Robert Hull, Raintree Steck-Vaughn 1998
WHAT DO WE KNOW ABOUT THE GREEKS?
by Anne Pearson, Peter Bedrick Books 1992
FIRST FACTS ABOUT THE ANCIENT GREEKS
by Fiona Macdonald, Peter Bedrick Books 1997

Books for older readers:

OXFORD HISTORY OF THE CLASSICAL WORLD, edited by John Boardman et al., Oxford University Press 1986
THE WORLD OF ODYSSEUS, revised edition, by M.I. Finley, The Viking Press 1978
EVERYDAY THINGS IN ANCIENT GREECE by Marjorie and C.H.B. Quennell, revised by Kathleen Freeman, G.P. Putnam's Sons 1954

Index